T0113918

90 IN 90

A 90-DAY DAILY DEVOTIONAL

FOR CHRISTIANS IN RECOVERY

Robert Lambert

WESTBOW
PRESS®
A DIVISION OF THOMAS NELSON
& ZONDERVAN

WestBow Press books may be ordered through booksellers or by contacting:

WestBow Press
A Division of Thomas Nelson & Zondervan
1663 Liberty Drive
Bloomington, IN 47403
www.westbowpress.com
844-714-3454

ISBN: 978-1-6642-4911-0 (sc)
ISBN: 978-1-6642-4910-3 (e)

Print information available on the last page.

WestBow Press rev. date: 11/19/2021

WHY THIS DAILY DEVOTIONAL?

If you're anything like me, then you have a sponsor who always tells you to *read about this* and *write about that*. I mean, hey, it's what we do in 12-step recovery, right? We **uncover** so that we can **discover**, in order to **recover**! That's just how it works!

In addition to all the reading and writing, I was always told to look up words. Not only the words I don't know, but also the words I think I know. Corny! That's exactly what I thought when I first heard someone suggest it. But I have to be honest, it revolutionized my thought process and ability to learn. Many years later, as a Christian studying the Bible, I have continued to do the same.

Another vital lesson I learned in my thirty-plus years in 12-step recovery was this: I need to experience evidence, truth, and God for myself. It just isn't enough to listen to others share and hope to identify. Recovery is a personal journey, and freedom is found in the experience.

I have discovered that learning God's word and His will for my life as a Christian is no different. It is a personal journey with personal experiences! I quickly discovered that I couldn't just read a verse and think about what it meant to me; I had to dig in! As I dug deep into His word, I began to see the many ways 12-step recovery paralleled the Bible...WOW!

This 90-day devotional illustrates various topics that are common in 12-step recovery, using recovery language. Definitions to selected words are also provided to enhance your understanding of the message. Lastly, the message is connected to a verse in the Bible.

Open your Bible and, as you read each verse, answer these three questions: Who was speaking? Who were they speaking to? Why were they speaking about this?

I hope you enjoy your 90-day journey!

Contact Information

"I have an enemy who is Cunning, Baffling, and Insidious"

Enemy: A opposing force, seeking to cause harm.
Cunning: Slick and crafty, with keen insight.
Baffling: Exceedingly confusing, disorienting and blurring.
Insidious: Gradually causing harm that is not easily noticed. Harmful yet enticing.

Genesis 3:1

_____

_____

_____

_____

_____

_____

_____

_____

_____

_____

_____

_____

_____

_____

1

"My best thinking led me down a path of destruction"

My: Saying that something belongs to you.

Best: Highest quality.

Thinking: Using your mind to understand, make judgments decisions, and solve problems.

Led: (lead) To conduct or direct with authority.

Path: A set of actions that lead to a result.

Destruction: Damage to something so bad, it no longer exists.

Proverbs 3:5,6

_____

_____

_____

_____

_____

_____

_____

_____

_____

_____

_____

_____

_____

_____

_____

_____

2

"If my 3rd step decision has no action... it's only a thought"

Decision: A choice one makes.
Has: Possess, experience.
No: Not any.
Action: Something done, performed.
Only: Nothing more.
Thought: An idea or notion.

James 2:26

3

"Hocus-Pocus, keep the focus"

Keep: Retain, continue in a specified condition.
Focus: The center of attention, attraction, or activity.

Matthew 7:3-5

_____
_____
_____
_____
_____
_____
_____
_____
_____
_____
_____
_____
_____
_____
_____
_____
_____
_____
_____
_____
_____

4

"My Recovery is a Gift"

My: Indicates possession.
Recovery: Regaining that which was lost. Returning to normal.
Gift: Something given voluntarily, especially to show affection.

Titus 3:5

_____
_____
_____
_____
_____
_____
_____
_____
_____
_____
_____
_____
_____
_____
_____
_____
_____
_____
_____

_____

"My character defects took me, kept me, and cost me..."

Character: The nature or qualities distinctive to a person.
Defects: Abnormalities, causing one not to function properly.
Took: (Take) Capture, move someone somewhere.
Kept: Continue in a specific condition or on a specific course.
Cost: A sacrifice that must be made.

James 1:14,15

_____
_____
_____
_____
_____
_____
_____
_____
_____
_____
_____
_____
_____
_____
_____
_____

6

"My gratitude speaks when I serve others"

<u>Gratitude:</u> Grateful, thankful, awakened by a favor received.
<u>Speaks:</u> Demonstrates, shows.
<u>Serve:</u> To perform duties, give aid, help or assistance.
<u>Others:</u> A person or group different from oneself.

Galatians 5:13,14

_____
_____
_____
_____
_____
_____
_____
_____
_____
_____
_____
_____
_____
_____
_____
_____

_____

"I know my God is loving and caring"

Know: Understand as fact or truth.
God: The one supreme being.
Loving: Showing profound, tender affection.
Caring: Displaying kindness, concern for others.

Romans 5:8

_____
_____
_____
_____
_____
_____
_____
_____
_____
_____
_____
_____
_____
_____
_____
_____
_____
_____

"Stay vigilant!"

<u>Stay:</u> Continue, remain in a place or condition.
<u>Vigilant:</u> Staying alert. Keeping careful watch for danger.

Matthew 24:44

_____

_____

_____

_____

_____

_____

_____

_____

_____

_____

_____

_____

_____

_____

_____

_____

_____

_____

_____

9

"Whatever the day brings…"

<u>Whatever:</u> No matter what.
<u>Day:</u> Twenty-four hours.
<u>Brings:</u> Conduct, convey or cause.

Hebrews 13:8

10

"Fear is at the root of my character defects"

Fear: A disturbing emotion caused by impending danger whether real or imagined.

At: Indicates a place.

Root: The origin or source of something.

Character: The nature of a person.

Defects: An abnormality that causes a person not to function properly.

1 John 4:18

_____
_____
_____
_____
_____
_____
_____
_____
_____
_____
_____
_____
_____
_____

_____

"Came to believe"

Came: Arrive to a condition, state, or position.
To: Expressing direction toward something approached and reached.
Believe: Accept as true.

Hebrews 11:6

_____
_____
_____
_____
_____
_____
_____
_____
_____
_____
_____
_____
_____
_____
_____
_____
_____
_____

12

_____

"But for the grace of God..."

But: Indicates the impossibility of anything other than what is being stated.
Grace: The unmerited, underserved favor of God.
God: Creator, ruler, supreme being.

Ephesians 2:8,9

_____
_____
_____
_____
_____
_____
_____
_____
_____
_____
_____
_____
_____
_____
_____
_____
_____
_____

13

"Carry the message"

Carry: To transport from one place to another.
Message: Communication containing a central point, theme, or idea.

Mark 1:7

14

"We continued to take a
personal inventory..."

Continued: Maintaining, enduring without interruption.
Personal: Related to and affecting you, not anyone else.
Inventory: A detailed list of all things.

2 Corinthians 13:5

15

"Unity is a must"

<u>Unity:</u> Being in harmony or one spirit.
<u>Must:</u> Not to be overlooked, necessary.

Matthew 5:9

16

"God is my greatest source of strength and courage"

God: Supreme being.
Greatest: First, best, superior.
Source: The origin from which something comes.
Strength: State of being strong. Moral power, firmness.
Courage: The ability of facing or dealing with anything recognized as dangerous, difficult, or painful, instead of withdrawing from it.

Deuteronomy 31:6

_____
_____
_____
_____
_____
_____
_____
_____
_____
_____
_____
_____
_____
_____
_____

_____

"My recovery starts at home"

Recovery: The process of returning to a normal state.
Starts: The point at which something originates.
Home: The place where one lives.

Mark 5:19

_____
_____
_____
_____
_____
_____
_____
_____
_____
_____
_____
_____
_____
_____
_____
_____
_____
_____

"Alone, I am in bad company"

Alone: Having no one, on one's own.
In: Contained.
Bad: Not good, unpleasant, causing difficulty or harm.
Company: The condition of being/associating with another.

Hebrews 10:24,25

_____

_____

_____

_____

_____

_____

_____

_____

_____

_____

_____

_____

_____

_____

_____

_____

_____

_____

19

"Asking God for wisdom improves my understanding of the steps"

Asking: To request.

Wisdom: Discernment, insight, knowing what is true and right.

Improves: Becomes better.

Understanding: The ability to comprehend, to grasp the meaning or significance of something.

James 1:5

_____

_____

_____

_____

_____

_____

_____

_____

_____

_____

_____

_____

_____

_____

"I can't... He can... Let Him"

Can't: No ability, unable.
Can: To have the ability, power, or skill.
Let: To give permission or opportunity, allow.

James 4:6-10

21

"I became entirely ready..."

Became: Develop or progress into.
Entirely: Wholly, completely, unreservedly.
Ready: Prepared.

Ephesians 4:22,23

"Today- When I am wrong,
I will promptly admit it"

When: In the event that.
Wrong: Incorrect, untrue, unjust, immoral.
Promptly: Prepared.
Admit: Embrace as the truth.

1 John 1:8-10

_____
_____
_____
_____
_____
_____
_____
_____
_____
_____
_____
_____
_____
_____
_____
_____
_____

23

"I humbly ask Him..."

<u>Humbly:</u> Not proud, haughty, or arrogant.
<u>Ask:</u> Request, inquire, invite.
<u>Him:</u> referring to God.

1 John 5:14,15

_____
_____
_____
_____
_____
_____
_____
_____
_____
_____
_____
_____
_____
_____
_____
_____
_____
_____

24

"God is with me, ready to help... if I call on Him"

With: One with another, together.
Ready: Fully prepared.
Help: To give or provide what is necessary.
If: In the event of.
Call: Cry out.

Psalm 120:1

_____

_____

_____

_____

_____

_____

_____

_____

_____

_____

_____

_____

_____

_____

_____

_____

_____

25

_____

"A humbled heart is key to this new way of life"

Humbled: Made less proud, especially by gratitude for help received, undeserved advantage.
Heart: The center or inner most part of a person.
Key: Crucial, paramount.

Matthew 23:12

_____
_____
_____
_____
_____
_____
_____
_____
_____
_____
_____
_____
_____
_____
_____
_____
_____
_____

"Take my will and my life..."

Take: Assume possession or control.
Will: A person's wishes, decisions.
Life: A person's every day affairs.

Matthew 16:24

27

"Freedom is found in the pause"

Freedom: The condition of not being under the control of another power.
Found: Discovered, based in the belief.
Pause: Temporarily stop.

Psalm 46:10

_____
_____
_____
_____
_____
_____
_____
_____
_____
_____
_____
_____
_____
_____
_____
_____
_____

28

"And then something happens"

Then: Points to a moment in time.
Something: Refers to a situation.
Happens: To occur or take place.

Psalm 9:9,10

29

"Each voyage starts with the first step"

Each: Every, all.
Voyage: A passage or course from one stage to another.
Starts: Begin to occur or take place.
First: Points to origination or starting point.
Step: One part in a process.

Luke 13:18,19

"Step 8, doing my part to help others heal"

Help: Contribute something that makes it easier to deal with a problem.
Others: People other than myself.
Heal: Relieve or alleviate one's anguish or distress.

Matthew 5:23,24

_____
_____
_____
_____
_____
_____
_____
_____
_____
_____
_____
_____
_____
_____
_____
_____
_____
_____

"Embracing my powerlessness"

Embracing: To receive gladly, to welcome or accept willingly.
Powerlessness: Without ability, strength, or authority.

2 Corinthians 12:9

_____

_____

_____

_____

_____

_____

_____

_____

_____

_____

_____

_____

_____

_____

_____

_____

_____

_____

_____

_____

"If you want what I have, do what I do"

<u>If:</u> In the event of.
<u>Want:</u> Have need or desire, wish for.
<u>Do:</u> Perform or achieve an exact action.

1 Corinthians 11:1

33

_____

"Generosity is a spiritual principle"

Generosity: The willingness to give or share.
Spiritual: Matters of the soul.
Principle: A rule, truth or belief that guides.

2 Corinthians 9:7

_____
_____
_____
_____
_____
_____
_____
_____
_____
_____
_____
_____
_____
_____
_____
_____
_____
_____

"God grant me serenity"

<u>God:</u> Supreme being.
<u>Grant:</u> Give something requested.
<u>Serenity:</u> State of calmness and peace.

Isaiah 26:3

_____
_____
_____
_____
_____
_____
_____
_____
_____
_____
_____
_____
_____
_____
_____
_____
_____
_____
_____

"God grant me courage"

God: Supreme being.
Grant: Give something requested.
Courage: Strength to proceed, persevere in the midst of fear or difficulty.

Joshua 1:9

_____
_____
_____
_____
_____
_____
_____
_____
_____
_____
_____
_____
_____
_____
_____
_____
_____
_____
_____

"God grant me wisdom"

God: Supreme being.

Grant: Give something requested.

Wisdom: The ability to have good judgement and make sound decisions.

Proverbs 2:6

———————————————
———————————————
———————————————
———————————————
———————————————
———————————————
———————————————
———————————————
———————————————
———————————————
———————————————
———————————————
———————————————
———————————————
———————————————
———————————————
———————————————
———————————————
———————————————

_____

"Keep putting one foot in front of the other"

Keep: Continue in a particular condition or on a particular course.

Galatians 6:9

_____
_____
_____
_____
_____
_____
_____
_____
_____
_____
_____
_____
_____
_____
_____
_____
_____
_____

"The use of a substance is merely a symptom"

Use: Take to achieve a result.
Substance: Drugs, alcohol, sex, gambling, porn, etc.
Symptom: Subjective evidence of a disorder or undesirable situation.

Mark 7:21,22

_____
_____
_____
_____
_____
_____
_____
_____
_____
_____
_____
_____
_____
_____
_____
_____
_____

39

"Just for today"

<u>Just:</u> Only, simply.
<u>Today:</u> Twenty-four hours.

Matthew 6:34

_____
_____
_____
_____
_____
_____
_____
_____
_____
_____
_____
_____
_____
_____
_____
_____
_____
_____

40

"Restore me to sanity"

Restore: Bring back to the original condition.
Sanity: Soundness, rational, and reasonable.

Daniel 4:36

41

"Religion is not a relationship"

Religion: A set of practices based on a particular belief.
Not: A word used for denying.
Relationship: A close connection between two people.

Matthew 15:8

42

"Thank God I didn't get
what I deserve"

Thank: Used to express gratitude for something someone has done.
Get: Receive, acquire.
Deserve: To have earned.

Romans 6:23

_____
_____
_____
_____
_____
_____
_____
_____
_____
_____
_____
_____
_____
_____
_____
_____
_____

43

_____

"Having a spiritual awakening"

Having: Possessing, experiencing.
Spiritual: Relating to the soul.
Awakening: The process of waking from sleep, becoming aware.

John 6:29

_____
_____
_____
_____
_____
_____
_____
_____
_____
_____
_____
_____
_____
_____
_____
_____
_____

44

"In times of trouble"

Times: The period a condition exists.
Trouble: Problems, worry, distress, pain, etc.

Isaiah 41:10

_____
_____
_____
_____
_____
_____
_____
_____
_____
_____
_____
_____
_____
_____
_____
_____
_____
_____
_____

45

"My real worth can be found in just being me"

Real: Not fake, false, or artificial.
Worth: The level at which someone deserves to be valued.
Found: To base a belief, claim or idea on something.
Being: Living as.

Galatians 1:10

_____
_____
_____
_____
_____
_____
_____
_____
_____
_____
_____
_____
_____
_____
_____

"Honesty"

<u>Honesty:</u> Absence of deceit or fraud.

Proverbs 10:9

"Open-minded"

Open: Allowing access, without a limit or boundary.
Minded: Having a particular way of thinking.

Romans 12:2

_____
_____
_____
_____
_____
_____
_____
_____
_____
_____
_____
_____
_____
_____
_____
_____
_____
_____

"Pray to become Willing"

Pray: To speak to God.
Become: Grow to be, come to be, change.
Willing: Heartily or ungrudgingly consenting.

Ezekiel 36:26

_____
_____
_____
_____
_____
_____
_____
_____
_____
_____
_____
_____
_____
_____
_____
_____
_____
_____
_____
_____

"I must remain vigilant"

Must: Necessary, under obligation.
Remain: Stay with, continue.
Vigilant: Aware and attentively watchful.

1 Peter 5:8

_____
_____
_____
_____
_____
_____
_____
_____
_____
_____
_____
_____
_____
_____
_____
_____
_____
_____

50

"Feelings are not facts. Therefore, I will walk in the truth"

<u>Feelings:</u> Emotionally perceiving.
<u>Facts:</u> Known to be the truth.
<u>Therefore:</u> Because of that reason.
<u>Walk:</u> Put one foot in front of the other.
<u>Truth:</u> That which is in agreement with, fact.

2 Corinthians 5:7

51

"My thinking is upside-down"

Thinking: The way I process information.
Upside-down: With much confusion, twisted.

Romans 8:7

_____
_____
_____
_____
_____
_____
_____
_____
_____
_____
_____
_____
_____
_____
_____
_____
_____
_____
_____

(F.A.T.)
"Am I faithful?"

Faithful: Steadfast, devoted, and loyal in my allegiance to God.

1 John 2:24,25

_____
_____
_____
_____
_____
_____
_____
_____
_____
_____
_____
_____
_____
_____
_____
_____
_____
_____
_____
_____
_____

(F.A.T.)
"Am I available?"

<u>Available:</u> Not presently involved or occupied, able to be employed for a purpose.

Mark 1:16-18

(F.A.T.)
"Am I still teachable?"

<u>Still:</u> Even at the present moment.
<u>Teachable:</u> When one is able and willing to be taught.

Proverbs 29:1

_____
_____
_____
_____
_____
_____
_____
_____
_____
_____
_____
_____
_____
_____
_____
_____
_____
_____
_____

"Think about what you think about"

Think: Consider, ponder.
About: Regarding, concerning.

Philippians 4:8

_____
_____
_____
_____
_____
_____
_____
_____
_____
_____
_____
_____
_____
_____
_____
_____
_____
_____
_____
_____
_____

"Change will not come by
hearing alone, I must do!"

Change: Become something different, new.
Hearing: Listening to ourselves or others.
Alone: Solely by itself.
Do: Take action, live out.

James 1:23-25

_____
_____
_____
_____
_____
_____
_____
_____
_____
_____
_____
_____
_____
_____
_____

"I'm Looking at the person in the Mirror"

Looking: Inventorying.
Person: Me, myself, and I.
Mirror: Reflection, truth.

Psalm 139:23,24

_____

_____

_____

_____

_____

_____

_____

_____

_____

_____

_____

_____

_____

_____

_____

_____

_____

"Just one…is too many"

Is: Present time.
Too: More than desirable.
Many: A great amount.

John 8:34

_____
_____
_____
_____
_____
_____
_____
_____
_____
_____
_____
_____
_____
_____
_____
_____
_____
_____
_____

"Seeking approval will only divert me from my primary purpose"

Seeking: Asking, desiring, attempting to gain.
Approval: Acceptance.
Divert: Shift away from a designated destination.
Purpose: The reason I was created.

John 12:43

_____
_____
_____
_____
_____
_____
_____
_____
_____
_____
_____
_____
_____
_____
_____

CONGRATULATIONS! SHOW UP TO GROW UP!

"I have to be honest about where I'm really at"

I: Me.
Honest: Straightforward and transparent.
Really: Sincerely and truly.
At: Indicates my spiritual condition.

Mark 9:24

_____
_____
_____
_____
_____
_____
_____
_____
_____
_____
_____
_____
_____
_____
_____
_____
_____

_____

"I've come to realize I am sick"

<u>I've:</u> I have.
<u>Realize:</u> To grasp clearly.
<u>Sick:</u> Affected by illness.

Mark 2:17

_____
_____
_____
_____
_____
_____
_____
_____
_____
_____
_____
_____
_____
_____
_____
_____
_____
_____
_____

"To those who relapse and return... special encouragement"

Relapse: Wander off, back into a bad condition.
Return: To come back.
Special: Extra.
Encouragement: Inspiration or praise.

Matthew 18:12-14

"Sometimes we get our needs and wants mixed up"

<u>Sometimes:</u> On occasion.
<u>Needs:</u> Absolutely required.
<u>Wants:</u> To desire things that are not absolutely required.
<u>Mixed:</u> Confused.

Philippians 4:19

_____
_____
_____
_____
_____
_____
_____
_____
_____
_____
_____
_____
_____
_____
_____
_____
_____

_____

"Today I have hope"

Today: Now.
Have: Possess.
Hope: Looking forward with confidence.

Romans 8:24,25

_____
_____
_____
_____
_____
_____
_____
_____
_____
_____
_____
_____
_____
_____
_____
_____
_____
_____

65

"Does it need to be said?
Does it need to be said now?
Does it need to be said by me?"

Does: Ought, should.
Need: Necessary or required.
Said: Communicated or spoken.

Proverbs 15:2

_____
_____
_____
_____
_____
_____
_____
_____
_____
_____
_____
_____
_____
_____
_____
_____
_____

66

"The only suggestions I pay for, are the ones I don't take"

Suggestion: An idea to consider, proposal.
Only: Exclusively.
Pay: Suffer the consequence.
Take: Receive and apply.

Proverbs 19:20

_____
_____
_____
_____
_____
_____
_____
_____
_____
_____
_____
_____
_____
_____
_____
_____
_____
_____

"Grateful for the gift of the moment"

Grateful: Feelings of appreciation and thankfulness.
Gift: Something I've been given yet did not earn.
Moment: Now, the present.

Ecclesiastes 6:9

_____
_____
_____
_____
_____
_____
_____
_____
_____
_____
_____
_____
_____
_____
_____
_____
_____
_____

"Which is better...to be right or to be happy?"

Better: Greater, more superior than something.
Right: Correct, aligning with fact or truth.
Happy: Feeling content, pleased or glad.

Proverbs 17:19

_____

_____

_____

_____

_____

_____

_____

_____

_____

_____

_____

_____

_____

_____

_____

_____

_____

_____

"I have a choice"

Have: Own, possess.
Choice: The freedom of selecting, or deciding, when given more than one option.

Joshua 24:15

_____

_____

_____

_____

_____

_____

_____

_____

_____

_____

_____

_____

_____

_____

_____

_____

_____

70

"Keep it simple"

<u>Keep:</u> Do something without ceasing.
<u>Simple:</u> Uncomplicated and plain.

Ecclesiastes 7:29

_____
_____
_____
_____
_____
_____
_____
_____
_____
_____
_____
_____
_____
_____
_____
_____
_____
_____
_____
_____

"I can't do this alone"

<u>This:</u> My recovery.
<u>Alone:</u> By myself, entirely separated.

Ecclesiastes 4:10

"People, Places and Things"

People: Men, women, and children.
Places: Particular areas or locations.
Things: Material objects too numerous to name.

Matthew 7:13

_____
_____
_____
_____
_____
_____
_____
_____
_____
_____
_____
_____
_____
_____
_____
_____
_____
_____

"It is by God's grace and mercy..."

By: Because of.

God: The supreme being.

Grace: Favor I did not earn, and do not deserve.

Mercy: Compassion and kindness given from one in power toward the offender.

Hebrews 4:16

_____

_____

_____

_____

_____

_____

_____

_____

_____

_____

_____

_____

_____

_____

_____

_____

_____

_____

"Humility...an ideal state"

<u>Humility:</u> Pride and arrogance free.
<u>Ideal:</u> Perfect, model, suitable.
<u>State:</u> A certain condition.

1 Corinthians 4:7

_____
_____
_____
_____
_____
_____
_____
_____
_____
_____
_____
_____
_____
_____
_____
_____
_____
_____
_____

_____

"The power that brought me here is still with me"

Power: Authority and means to control.
Brought: To carry or cause.
Still: Remains, even now.
With: Accompanying, together.

Hebrews 13:8

_____
_____
_____
_____
_____
_____
_____
_____
_____
_____
_____
_____
_____
_____
_____
_____

"God will not force Himself on us"

God: The ultimate authority.

Force: Strength exerted on another to make them do something against their will.

Himself: Emphasizes the one previously mentioned.

Revelation 3:20

_____

_____

_____

_____

_____

_____

_____

_____

_____

_____

_____

_____

_____

_____

_____

_____

_____

_____

_____

"When my defects have me weary"

When: What point in time something occurs.
Defects: A flaw in one's character that affects performance.
Have: In a position of.
Weary: To become very tired of something, exhausted.

Matthew 11:28,29

_____
_____
_____
_____
_____
_____
_____
_____
_____
_____
_____
_____
_____
_____
_____
_____

"Gratitude for my predecessors"

<u>Gratitude:</u> Thankful, appreciative.
<u>Predecessors:</u> Those who were here before me.

Leviticus 19:22

_____
_____
_____
_____
_____
_____
_____
_____
_____
_____
_____
_____
_____
_____
_____
_____
_____
_____
_____

"Pride has a way of leading me into celebrating myself"

Pride: An exaggerated, high opinion of oneself, taking credit.
Way: Process, method.
Leading: Directing, enticing.
Celebrating: Observe with a ceremony or an occasion.

Luke 18:9

80

"I need a real God in the 2nd step
to show His real power in the 7th"

Real: An exaggerated, high opinion of oneself, taking credit.
Show: Process, method.
Power: Directing, enticing.

Job 26:7-14

_____
_____
_____
_____
_____
_____
_____
_____
_____
_____
_____
_____
_____
_____
_____
_____
_____
_____
_____

"I no longer have only spiritual theories"

No longer: Formally the case, but no more.
Only: Not anything more.
Spiritual: Relating to spiritual matters.
Theories: Ideas based on a belief that may lack personal experience.

Hebrews 7:25

_____

_____

_____

_____

_____

_____

_____

_____

_____

_____

_____

_____

_____

_____

"Freedom from the bondage of addiction"

Freedom: No longer a prisoner, slave.
Bondage: Subjected to a power greater than yourself.
Addiction: Repeated involvement with a substance or activity, despite the substantial harm it causes.

Romans 6:6

_____
_____
_____
_____
_____
_____
_____
_____
_____
_____
_____
_____
_____
_____
_____
_____
_____
_____
_____

_____

"Praying only for knowledge of..."

Praying: Speaking too, asking God.
Only: Nothing more, solely.
His: He, God, the one you are praying to.
Knowledge: Awareness, understanding.

Psalm 25:4,5

_____
_____
_____
_____
_____
_____
_____
_____
_____
_____
_____
_____
_____
_____
_____
_____

84

"…And the will to carry it out"

Will: Desire, want.
Carry: Comply, to do.
It: His will.

2 Thessalonians 1:11

_____
_____
_____
_____
_____
_____
_____
_____
_____
_____
_____
_____
_____
_____
_____
_____
_____
_____
_____

85

"I am no longer the person I used to be"

Am: Be.

No longer: What was once the truth, now is not.

Person: An individual with certain attributes.

Be: Live, exist.

2 Corinthians 5:17

"A strength that is not my own"

Strength: Power, courage, firmness.
Not: To deny.
My own: To acknowledge source or ownership.

Ephesians 3:16

_____
_____
_____
_____
_____
_____
_____
_____
_____
_____
_____
_____
_____
_____
_____
_____
_____
_____

"Practice these principles in all my affairs"

Practice: Do repeatedly.
Principles: Foundational truths that guide a belief and behavior.
All: Every, complete.
Affairs: Events and interactions, life.

Galatians 5:22

_____
_____
_____
_____
_____
_____
_____
_____
_____
_____
_____
_____
_____
_____
_____

"It didn't have to be this way"

<u>It:</u> My life, circumstances, situation.
<u>Didn't:</u> Did not, opposite of did.
<u>Have to:</u> To say something was necessary or required.
<u>Be:</u> Occur, be done, take place.

1 Peter 2:9

_____
_____
_____
_____
_____
_____
_____
_____
_____
_____
_____
_____
_____
_____
_____
_____
_____

_____

"Each one, Reach one, Teach one"

Each: Every and all.
Reach: Extend yourself.
Teach: Instruct, explain, to share your knowledge.

Matthew 28:18-20

_____
_____
_____
_____
_____
_____
_____
_____
_____
_____
_____
_____
_____
_____
_____
_____
_____
_____
_____
_____

ABOUT THE AUTHOR

Rob Lambert is a gifted communicator and leader at the Recovery House of Worship (RHOW) Bronx church. His love for Christ, coupled with compassion and the enthusiasm to reach and serve the recovery community, has led him to impact people across the country and around the globe.

Rob was born in Brockton, Massachusetts, to parents who were tormented by substance abuse. As a result, he started down the same path at the tender age of eleven.

In 1988, while caught in the grips of a crack cocaine addiction, Rob attended his first 12-step recovery meeting. After a struggle to maintain long-term clean time, he finally became free from drugs in 2005. However, his flesh continued to lead him down a road of destruction, ravaging his life and the lives of those around him. Except now, he couldn't blame the drugs!

In 2009, with four years clean and desperately searching for something greater than himself—his Higher Power--Rob left Massachusetts. He moved into the Recovery House of Worship (RHOW) in Brooklyn, New York, to participate in the Faith-Based Men's Recovery Program. Shortly after, he surrendered his life to Christ!

Since 2009, Rob has faithfully served in various ministries with RHOW Brooklyn, Bronx, and online churches.

In 2013, Rob completed a three-year Certification Program in Pastoral Theology from Urban Academy (URBACAD) and is a passionate student of the Word.

He is a singer/songwriter, actor, and playwright, most noted for the off-Broadway musical "Born in Brockton Born Again in Brooklyn."

Rob is married to Wanda, who supports him unconditionally by being the ministry "behind the scenes." They have a beautiful dog named Nāhgee, a bunch of nieces and nephews, and a never-ending love for Jesus, pizza, and ice cream.

Printed in the United States
by Baker & Taylor Publisher Services